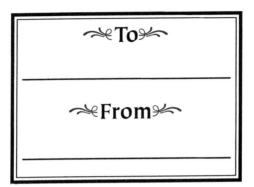

To
_____

From
_____

Cover design:
James C. Romano II

Page design:
Jeanne-Marie Sturz

Published by Chain Sales Marketing, Inc.
149 Madison Avenue, Suite #810
New York, NY 10016

in association with

Platinum Press
311 Crossways Park Drive
Woodbury, New York 11797

ISBN 1-55836-195-2

0 9 8 7 6 5 4 3 2 1

A
Book
of
Proverbs

1

1 The proverbs of Solomon
the son of David, king of Israel;

2 To know wisdom
and instruction; to perceive
the words of understanding;

3 To receive the instruction
of wisdom, justice,
and judgment, and equity;

4 To give subtilty to the simple,
to the young man knowledge
and discretion.

5 A wise man will hear, and will
increase learning; and a man of
understanding shall attain unto
wise counsels:

6 To understand a proverb, and the
interpretation; the words of the
wise, and their dark sayings.

Proverbs ❧ 1

7 The fear of the LORD is the beginning of knowledge: but fools despise wisdom and instruction.

❧

8 My son, hear the instruction of thy father, and forsake not the law of thy mother:

❧

9 For they shall be an ornament of grace unto thy head, and chains about thy neck.

❧

10 My son, if sinners entice thee, consent thou not.

❧

11 If they say, Come with us, let us lay wait for blood, let us lurk privily for the innocent without cause:

❧

12 Let us swallow them up alive as the grave; and whole, as those that go down into the pit:

Proverbs ❦ 1

13 We shall find all precious substance,
we shall fill our houses with spoil:

❦

14 Cast in thy lot among us;
let us all have one purse:

❦

15 My son, walk not thou
in the way with them;
refrain thy foot from their path:

❦

16 For their feet run to evil, and make
haste to shed blood.

❦

17 Surely in vain the net
is spread in the sight of any bird.

❦

18 And they lay wait for
their own blood; they lurk
privily for their own lives.

❦

19 So are the ways of every one
that is greedy of gain;
which taketh away the life
of the owners thereof.

Proverbs ❧ *1*

20 **W**isdom crieth without;
she uttereth her voice in the streets:

❧

21 **S**he crieth in the chief place
of concourse, in the openings
of the gates: in the city
she uttereth her words, saying,

❧

22 **H**ow long, ye simple ones,
will ye love simplicity?
and the scorners delight
in their scorning, and fools
hate knowledge?

❧

23 **T**urn you at my reproof: behold,
I will pour out my spirit unto you,
I will make known my words unto you.

❧

24 **B**ecause I have called, and ye
refused; I have stretched out my
hand, and no man regarded;

❧

25 **B**ut ye have set at nought all my
counsel, and would none of my reproof:

Proverbs ❧ 1

26 I also will laugh at your calamity;
I will mock when your fear cometh;

27 When your fear cometh as
desolation, and your destruction
cometh as a whirlwind;
when distress and anguish
cometh upon you.

28 Then shall they call upon me, but
I will not answer; they shall seek
me early, but they shall not find me:

29 For that they hated knowledge, and did
not choose the fear of the LORD:

30 They would none of my counsel:
they despised all my reproof.

31 Therefore shall they eat of the fruit of their
own way, and be filled with their own devices.

32 For the turning away of the simple
shall slay them, and the prosperity
of fools shall destroy them.

33 But whoso hearkeneth unto me
shall dwell safely, and shall be
quiet from fear of evil.

2

1 My son, if thou wilt receive my words,
and hide my commandments with thee;

❧

2 So that thou incline thine ear
unto wisdom, and apply thine
heart to understanding;

❧

3 Yea, if thou criest after knowledge, and
liftest up thy voice for understanding;

❧

4 If thou seekest her as silver, and searchest
for her as for hid treasures;

❧

5 Then shalt thou understand the fear of
the LORD, and find the knowledge of God.

❧

6 For the LORD giveth wisdom: out of him
cometh knowledge and understanding.

Proverbs ❧ 2

7   He layeth up sound wisdom
for the righteous: he is a buckler
to them that walk uprightly.

❧

8   He keepeth the paths of judgment,
and preserveth the way of his saints

❧

9   Then shalt thou understand
righteousness, and judgment,
and equity; yea, every good path.

❧

10   When wisdom entereth into thine heart,
and knowledge is pleasant unto thy soul;

❧

11   Discretion shall preserve thee,
understanding shall keep thee:

❧

12   To deliver thee from the way
of the evil man, from the man
that speaketh froward things;

❧

13   Who leave the paths of uprightness,
to walk in the ways of darkness;

Proverbs ⚮ *2*

14 Who rejoice to do evil, and delight
in the frowardness of the wicked;

⚮

15 Whose ways are crooked,
and they froward in their paths:

⚮

16 To deliver thee from the strange woman,
even from the stranger which
flattereth with her words;

⚮

17 Which forsaketh the guide of her youth,
and forgetteth the covenant of her God.

⚮

18 For her house inclineth unto death,
and her paths unto the dead.

⚮

19 None that go unto her return
again, neither take they hold
of the paths of life.

⚮

20 That thou mayest walk in the
way of good men, and keep
the paths of the righteous.

Proverbs ❦ 2

21 For the upright shall dwell in the land, and the perfect shall remain in it.

❦

22 But the wicked shall be cut off from the earth, and the transgressor shall be rooted out of it.

3

1 My son, forget not my law; but let thine heart keep my commandments:

❦

2 For length of days, and long life, and peace, shall they add to thee.

❦

3 Let not mercy and truth forsake thee: bind them about thy neck; write them upon the table of thine heart:

❦

4 So shalt thou find favour and good understanding in the sight of God and man.

❦

5 Trust in the LORD with all thine heart; lean not unto thine own understanding.

Proverbs ❧ 3

6 In all thy ways acknowledge him,
and he shall direct thy paths.

❧

7 Be not wise in thine own eyes:
fear the LORD, and depart from evil.

❧

8 It shall be health to thy navel,
and marrow to thy bones.

❧

9 Honour the LORD with thy substance,
and with the first fruits of thine increase:

❧

10 So shall thy barns be filled
with plenty, and thy presses
shall burst out with new wine.

❧

11 My son, despise not the chastening
of the LORD; neither be weary of
his correction:

❧

12 For whom the LORD loveth he
correcteth; even as a father the son
in whom he delighteth.

Proverbs 3

13 Happy is the man that findeth wisdom,
and the man that getteth understanding.

15 For the merchandise of it is better
than the merchandise of silver,
and the gain thereof than fine gold.

15 She is more precious than rubies:
and all the things thou canst desire
are not to be compared unto her.

16 Length of days is in her right hand;
and in her left hand riches and honour.

17 Her ways are ways of pleasantness,
and all her paths are peace

18 She is a tree of life to them that lay hold
upon her: and happy is every one
that retaineth her.

19 The LORD by wisdom hath founded
the earth; by understanding hath
he established the heavens.

Proverbs ❦ 3

20 By his knowledge the depths are broken
up, and the clouds drop down the dew.

❦

21 My son, let not them depart from thine
eyes: keep sound wisdom and discretion:

❦

22 So shall they be life unto thy soul,
and grace to thy neck.

❦

23 Then shalt thou walk
in thy way safely,
and thy foot shall not stumble.

❦

24 When thou liest down, thou shalt
not be afraid: yea, thou shalt lie down,
and thy sleep shall be sweet.

❦

25 Be not afraid of sudden fear,
neither of the desolation of the
wicked, when it cometh.

❦

26 For the LORD shall be thy
confidence, and shall keep
thy foot from being taken.

Proverbs ❦ 3

27 Withhold not good from them
to whom it is due, when it is in
the power of thine hand to do it.

28 Say not unto thy neighbour, Go,
and come again, and to morrow I
will give; when thou hast it by thee.

29 Devise not evil against thy neighbour,
seeing he dwelleth securely by thee.

30 Strive not with a man without cause,
if he have done thee no harm.

31 Envy thou not the oppressor,
and choose none of his ways.

32 For the froward is abomination to the
LORD: but his secret is with the righteous.

33 The curse of the LORD is in the house
of the wicked: but he blesseth
the habitation of the just.

Proverbs ❦ 3

34 Surely he scorneth the scorners:
but he giveth grace unto the lowly.

❦

35 The wise shall inherit glory: but
shame shall be the promotion of fools.

4

1 Hear, ye children, the instruction of
a father; attend to know understanding.

❦

2 For I give you good doctrine,
forsake ye not my law.

❦

3 For I was my father's son, tender and
only beloved in the sight of my mother.

❦

4 He taught me also, and said unto
me, Let thine heart retain my words:
keep my commandments, and live.

❦

5 Get wisdom, get understanding:
forget it not; neither decline from
the words of my mouth.

Proverbs ☙ *4*

6 Forsake her not, and she shall
   preserve thee: love her, and she
   shall keep thee.

☙

7 Wisdom is the principal thing;
   therefore get wisdom: and with all
   thy getting get understanding.

☙

8 Exalt her, and she
   shall promote thee:
   she shall bring thee to honour,
   when thou dost embrace her

☙

9 She shall give to thine head
   an ornament of grace: a crown
   of glory shall she deliver to thee.

☙

10 Hear, O my son, and receive my
    sayings; and the years of thy life
    shall be many.

☙

11 I have taught thee
    in the way of wisdom;
    I have led thee in right paths.

Proverbs ❦ 4

12 When thou goest, thy steps shall
not be straitened; and when thou runnest,
thou shalt not stumble.

❦

13 Take fast hold of instruction;
let her not go: keep her; for she is thy life.

❦

14 Enter not into the path of the wicked,
and go not in the way of evil men.

❦

15 Avoid it, pass not by it,
turn from it, and pass away.

❦

16 For they sleep not, except they have
done mischief; and their sleep is taken
away, unless they cause some to fall.

❦

17 For they eat the bread of wickedness,
and drink the wine of violence.

❦

18 But the path of the just is as the shining
light, that shineth more and more
unto the perfect day.

Proverbs ❧ *4*

19 The way of the wicked is as darkness:
they know not at what they stumble.

❧

20 My son, attend to my words;
incline thine ear unto my sayings.

❧

21 Let them not depart from thine eyes;
keep them in the midst of thine heart.

❧

22 For they are life unto those that find
them, and health to all their flesh.

❧

23 Keep thy heart with all diligence;
for out of it are the issues of life.

❧

24 Put away from thee a froward mouth,
and perverse lips put far from thee.

❧

25 Let thine eyes look right on,
and let thine eyelids look
straight before thee.

Proverbs ❧ 4

26 Ponder the path of thy feet,
and let all thy ways be established.

❧

27 Turn not to the right hand nor to
the left: remove thy foot from evil.

5

1 My son, attend unto my wisdom, and
bow thine ear to my understanding:

❧

2 That thou mayest regard discretion,
and that thy lips may keep knowledge.

❧

3 For the lips of a strange woman drop as
a honeycomb, and her mouth is
smoother than oil:

❧

4 But her end is bitter as wormwood,
sharp as a two-edged sword.

❧

5 Her feet go down to death
her steps take hold on hell.

Proverbs ❧ 5

6 Lest thou shouldest ponder the path
of life, her ways are moveable,
that thou canst not know them.

❧

7 Hear me now therefore, O ye children;
depart not from the words of my mouth.

❧

8 Remove thy way far from her,
and come not nigh the door of her house:

❧

9 Lest thou give thine honour unto
others, and thy years unto the cruel:

❧

10 Lest strangers be filled with thy wealth;
thy labours be in the house of a stranger;

❧

11 And thou mourn at the last,
when thy flesh and thy body
are consumed,

❧

12 And say, How have I hated
instruction, and my heart
despised reproof;

13 And have not obeyed the voice of
my teachers, nor inclined mine ear
to them that instructed me;

❧

14 I was almost in all evil in the midst
of the congregation and assembly.

❧

15 Drink waters out of thine own cistern,
and running waters out of thine own well.

❧

16 Let thy fountains be dispersed abroad,
and rivers of waters in the streets.

❧

17 Let them be only thine own,
and not strangers' with thee.

❧

18 Let thy fountain be blessed:
and rejoice with the wife of thy youth.

❧

19 Let her be as the loving hind
and pleasant roe; let her breasts
satisfy thee at all times; and be thou
ravished always with her love.

Proverbs ❧ 5

20 And why wilt thou, my son,
   be ravished with a strange woman,
   and embrace the bosom of a stranger?

❧

21 For the ways of man are before the eyes
   of the LORD, and he pondereth all his
   goings.

❧

22 His own iniquities shall take the wicked
   himself, and he shall be holden
   with the cords of his sins.

❧

23 He shall die without instruction;
   and in the greatness of his folly
   he shall go astray.

6

1 My son, if thou be surety for thy
   friend, if thou hast stricken
   thy hand with a stranger,

❧

2 Thou art snared with the words
   of thy mouth, thou art taken
   with the words of thy mouth.

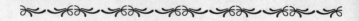

Proverbs ❦ 6

3 Do this now, my son, and deliver thyself,
   when thou art come into the hand
   of thy friend; go, humble thyself,
   and make sure thy friend.

   ❦

4 Give not sleep to thine eyes,
   nor slumber to thine eyelids.

   ❦

5 Deliver thyself as a roe from the hand
   of the hunter, and as a bird from
   the hand of the fowler.

   ❦

6 Go to the ant, thou sluggard;
   consider her ways, and be wise:

   ❦

7 Which having no guide,
   overseer, or ruler,

   ❦

8 Provideth her meat in the summer,
   and gathereth her food in the harvest.

   ❦

9 How long wilt thou sleep,
   O sluggard? When wilt thou
   arise out of thy sleep?

Proverbs 6

10 Yet a little sleep, a little slumber,
a little folding of the hands to sleep:

11 So shall thy poverty come as one that
travelleth, and thy want as an armed man.

12 A naughty person, a wicked man,
walketh with a froward mouth.

13 He winketh with his eyes, he speaketh
with his feet, he teacheth with his fingers;

14 Frowardness is in his heart,
he deviseth mischief continually;
he soweth discord.

15 Therefore shall his calamity
come suddenly; suddenly shall
he be broken without remedy.

16 These six things doth the
LORD hate: yea, seven are
an abomination unto him:

Proverbs ❧ 6

17 **A** proud look, a lying tongue, and
hands that shed innocent blood,

❧

18 **A** heart that deviseth wicked imaginations,
feet that be swift in running to mischief,

❧

19 **A** false witness that speaketh lies,
and he that soweth discord
among brethren.

❧

20 **M**y son, keep thy father's commandment,
and forsake not the law of thy mother:

❧

21 **B**ind them continually upon thine heart,
and tie them about thy neck.

❧

22 **W**hen thou goest, it shall lead thee;
when thou sleepest, it shall keep thee;
and when thou awakest,
it shall talk with thee.

❧

23 **F**or the commandment is a lamp;
and the law is light; and reproofs
of instruction are the way of life:

Proverbs ❧ 6

24 To keep thee from the evil woman,
from the flattery of the tongue
of a strange woman.

25 Lust not after her beauty in thine heart;
neither let her take thee with her eyelids.

26 For by means of a whorish woman a man
is brought to a piece of bread: and the
adultress will hunt for the precious life.

27 Can a man take fire in his bosom,
and his clothes not be burned?

28 Can one go upon hot coals,
and his feet not be burned?

29 So he that goeth in to
his neighbour's wife; whosoever
toucheth her shall not be innocent.

30 Men do not despise a thief, if he steal
to satisfy his soul when he is hungry;

31 But if he be found, he shall restore
sevenfold; he shall give all
the substance of his house.

☙

32 But whoso committeth adultery with a
woman lacketh understanding: he that
doeth it destroyeth his own soul.

☙

33 A wound and dishonour shall he get;
and his reproach shall not be wiped away.

☙

34 For jealousy is the rage of man: therefore
he will not spare in the day of vengeance.

☙

35 He will not regard any ransom;
neither will he rest content,
though thou givest many gifts.

7

1 My son, keep my words, and lay
up my commandments with thee.

☙

2 Keep my commandments, and live:
and my law as the apple of thine eye.

Proverbs ❧ 7

3 Bind them upon thy fingers, writ them
upon the table of thine heart.

❧

4 Say unto wisdom, Thou art my sister;
and call understanding thy kinswoman:

❧

5 That they may keep thee from the strange
woman, from the stranger which
flattereth with her words.

❧

6 For at the window of my house
I looked through my casement,

❧

7 And beheld among the simple ones,
I discerned among the youths,
a young man void of understanding,

❧

8 Passing through the street
near her corner; and he went
the way to her house,

❧

9 In the twilight, in the evening,
in the black and dark night:

Proverbs ❧ 7

10 And, behold, there met him a woman with
the attire of a harlot, and subtil of heart.

❧

11 She is loud and stubborn;
her feet abide not in her house:

❧

12 Now is she without, now in the streets,
and lieth in wait at every corner.

❧

13 So she caught him, and kissed him,
and with an impudent face
said unto him,

❧

14 I have peace offerings with me;
this day have I payed my vows.

❧

15 Therefore came I forth to meet thee,
diligently to seek thy face,
and I have found thee.

❧

16 I have decked my bed
with coverings of tapestry,
with carved works,
with fine linen of Egypt.

Proverbs ❦ *7*

17 I have perfumed my bed
with myrrh, aloes, and cinnamon.

❦

18 Come, let us take our fill of love until the
morning: let us solace ourselves with loves.

❦

19 For the goodman is not at home,
he is gone a long journey:

❦

20 He hath taken a bag of money with him,
and will come home at the day appointed.

❦

21 With her much fair speech
she caused him to yield, with the
flattering of her lips she forced him.

❦

22 He goeth after her straightway,
as an ox goeth to the slaughter,
or as a fool to the correction
of the stocks;

❦

23 Till a dart strike through his liver;
as a bird hasteth to the snare, and
knoweth not that it is for his life.

24 Hearken unto me now therefore,
O ye children, and attend to the
words of my mouth

❧

25 Let not thine heart decline to her
ways, go not astray in her paths.

❧

26 For she hath cast down many wounded:
many strong men have been slain by her.

❧

27 Her house is the way to hell, going
down to the chambers of death.

8

1 Doth not wisdom cry? and understanding
put forth her voice?

❧

2 She standeth in the top of high places,
by the way in the places of the paths.

❧

3 She crieth at the gates, at the entry
of the city, at the coming
in at the doors.

Proverbs ❦ 8

4 Unto you, O men, I call;
    and my voice is to the sons of man.

    ❦

5 O ye simple, understand wisdom:
    and, ye fools, be ye of
    an understanding heart.

    ❦

6 Hear; for I will speak of excellent things;
    and the opening of my lips
    shall be right things.

    ❦

7 For my mouth shall speak truth; and
    wickedness is an abomination to my lips.

    ❦

8 All the words of my mouth are in
    righteousness; there is nothing froward
    or perverse in them.

    ❦

9 They are all plain to him
    that understandeth, and right
    to them that find knowledge.

    ❦

10 Receive my instruction,
    and not silver; and knowledge
    rather than choice gold.

Proverbs ❦ 8

11 For wisdom is better than rubies;
and all the things that may be
desired are not to be compared to it.

❦

12 I wisdom dwell with prudence,
and find out knowledge of
witty inventions.

❦

13 The fear of the LORD
is to hate evil: pride, and arrogancy,
and the evil way, and the
froward mouth, do I hate.

❦

14 Counsel is mine, and sound wisdom:
I am understanding; I have strength.

❦

15 By me kings reign,
and princes decree justice.

❦

16 By me princes rule, and nobles,
even all the judges of the earth.

❦

17 I love them that love me; and those that
seek me early shall find me.

Proverbs ❦ 8

18 Riches and honour are with me;
yea, durable riches and righteousness.

❦

19 My fruit is better than gold, yea, than fine
gold; and my revenue than choice silver.

❦

20 I lead in the way of righteousness,
in the midst of the paths of judgment:

❦

21 That I may cause those that love me
to inherit substance;
and I will fill their treasures.

❦

22 The LORD possessed me in the beginning
of his way, before his works of old.

❦

23 I was set up from everlasting,
from the beginning,
or ever the earth was.

❦

24 When there were no depths,
I was brought forth;
when there were no fountains
abounding with water.

Proverbs 🐦 8

25 **B**efore the mountains were settled,
before the hills was I brought forth:

🐦

26 **W**hile as yet he had not made
the earth, nor the fields, nor the
highest part of the dust of the world.

🐦

27 **W**hen he prepared the heavens,
I was there: when he set a compass
upon the face of the depth:

🐦

28 **W**hen he established the clouds
above: when he strengthened
the fountains of the deep:

🐦

29 **W**hen he gave to the sea his decree,
that the waters should not pass his
commandment: when he appointed
the foundations of the earth:

🐦

30 **T**hen I was by him, as one brought
up with him: and I was daily his
delight, rejoicing always before him;

Proverbs ❧ 8

31 Rejoicing in the habitable part of his earth;
and my delights were with the sons of men.

❧

32 Now therefore hearken unto me,
O ye children: for blessed are the
that keep my ways.

❧

33 Hear instruction, and be wise,
and refuse it not.

❧

34 Blessed is the man that heareth me,
watching daily at my gates,
waiting at the posts of my doors.

❧

35 For whoso findeth me findeth life,
and shall obtain favour of the LORD.

❧

36 But he that sinneth against me wrongeth
his own soul: they that hate me love death.

9

1 Wisdom hath builded her house,
she hath hewn out her seven pillars:

Proverbs ☙ 9

2 **S**he hath killed her beasts;
she hath mingled her wine;
she hath also furnished her table.

☙

3 **S**he hath sent forth her maidens:
she crieth upon the highest
places of the city,

☙

4 **W**hoso is simple, let him turn in
hither: as for him that wanteth
understanding, she saith to him,

☙

5 **C**ome, eat of my bread, and drink of
the wine which I have mingled.

☙

6 **F**orsake the foolish, and live;
and go in the way of understanding.

☙

7 **H**e that reproveth a scorner getteth to
himself shame: and he that rebuketh
a wicked man getteth himself a blot.

☙

8 **R**eprove not a scorner, lest he hate thee:
rebuke a wise man, and he will love thee.

Proverbs ❧ 9

9 Give instruction to a wise man, and he
will be yet wiser: teach a just man,
and he will increase in learning.

❧

10 The fear of the LORD is the
beginning of wisdom: and the
knowledge of the holy is understanding.

❧

11 For by me thy days shall be multiplied,
and the years of thy life shall be increased.

❧

12 If thou be wise, thou shalt be wise
for thyself: but if thou scornest,
thou alone shalt bear it.

❧

13 A foolish woman is clamorous:
she is simple, and knoweth nothing.

❧

14 For she sitteth at the door of her house,
on a seat in the high places of the city,

❧

15 To call passengers who
go right on their ways:

Proverbs ❧ 9

16 **W**hoso is simple, let him turn in hither:
and as for him that wanteth
understanding, she saith to him,

❧

17 **S**tolen waters are sweet, and bread
eaten in secret is pleasant.

❧

18 **B**ut he knoweth not that the dead
are there; and that her guests
are in the depths of hell.

10

1 **T**he proverbs of Solomon.
A wise son maketh a glad father: but a
foolish son is the heaviness of his mother.

❧

2 **T**reasures of wickedness profit nothing:
but righteousness delivereth from death.

❧

3 **T**he LORD will not suffer
the soul of the righteous to famish:
but he casteth away the
substance of the wicked.

Proverbs ❧ *10*

4 He becometh poor that dealeth
with a slack hand: but the hand
of the diligent maketh rich.

❧

5 He that gathereth in summer
is a wise son: but he that sleepeth
in harvest is a son that causeth shame.

❧

6 Blessings are upon the head of the just:
but violence covereth
the mouth of the wicked.

❧

7 The memory of the just is blessed:
but the name of the wicked shall rot.

❧

8 The wise in heart will receive
commandments: but a prating fool
shall fall.

❧

9 He that walketh uprightly walketh surely:
but he that perverteth his ways shall be known.

❧

10 He that winketh with the eye causeth
sorrow: but a prating fool shall fall.

Proverbs ❧ 10

11 The mouth of a righteous man
is a well of life: but violence covereth
the mouth of the wicked.

❧

12 Hatred stirreth up strifes:
but love covereth all sins.

❧

13 In the lips of him that hath understanding
wisdom is found: but a rod is for the back
of him that is void of understanding.

❧

14 Wise men lay up knowledge: but the
mouth of the foolish is near destruction.

❧

15 The rich man's wealth is his strong city:
destruction of the poor is their poverty.

❧

16 The labour of the righteous tendeth to life:
the fruit of the wicked to sin.

❧

17 He is in the way of life
that keepeth instruction:
but he that refuseth reproof erreth.

Proverbs ❧ *10*

18 He that hideth hatred with lying lips,
and he that uttereth a slander, is a fool.

❧

19 In the multitude of words there wanteth
not sin: but he that refraineth
his lips is wise.

❧

20 The tongue of the just is as choice silver:
the heart of the wicked is little worth.

❧

21 The lips of the righteous feed many:
but fools die for want of wisdom.

❧

22 The blessing of the LORD, it maketh
rich, and he addeth no sorrow with it.

❧

23 It is as sport to a fool
to do mischief: but a man
of understanding hath wisdom.

❧

24 The fear of the wicked, it shall
come upon him: but the desire
of the righteous shall be granted.

Proverbs ☙ 10

25 As the whirlwind passeth, so is the wicked
no more: but the righteous is an
everlasting foundation.

☙

26 As vinegar to the teeth, and a smoke
to the eyes, so is the sluggard
to them that send him.

☙

27 The fear of the LORD prolongeth days: but
the years of the wicked shall be shortened.

☙

28 The hope of the righteous shall be
gladness: but the expectation
of the wicked shall perish.

☙

29 The way of the LORD is strength
to the upright: but destruction
shall be to the workers of iniquity.

☙

30 The righteous shall never be emoved: but
the wicked shall not inhabit the earth.

☙

31 The mouth of the just bringeth forth
wisdom: but the froward tongue
shall be cut out.

Proverbs ❧ *10*

32 The lips of the righteous know
what is acceptable: but the mouth
of the wicked speaketh frowardness.

11

1 A false balance is abomination to the
LORD: but a just weight is his delight.

❦

2 When pride cometh, then cometh
shame: but with the lowly is wisdom.

❦

3 The integrity of the upright shall
guide them: but the perverseness
of transgressors shall destroy them.

❦

4 Riches profit not in the day of wrath:
but righteousness delivereth from death.

❦

5 The righteousness of the perfect
shall direct his way: but the wicked
shall fall by his own wickedness.

Proverbs ❧ 11

6 The righteousness of the upright
shall deliver them: but transgressors
shall be taken in their own naughtiness.

❧

7 When a wicked man dieth, his
expectation shall perish: and the
hope of unjust men perisheth.

❧

8 The righteous is delivered out of trouble,
and the wicked cometh in his stead.

❧

9 A hypocrite with his mouth destroyeth
his neighbour: but through knowledge
shall the just be delivered.

❧

10 When it goeth well with the righteous,
the city rejoiceth: and when the wicked
perish, there is shouting.

❧

11 By the blessing of the upright
the city is exalted: but it is overthrown
by the mouth of the wicked.

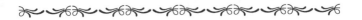

Proverbs ❧ 11

12 He that is void of wisdom despiseth
his neighbour: but a man of
understanding holdeth his peace.

13 A talebearer revealeth secrets: but he that
is of a faithful spirit concealeth the matter.

14 Where no counsel is, the people fall:
but in the multitude of counsellors
there is safety.

15 He that is surety for a stranger shall smart
for it: and he that hateth suretiship is sure.

16 A gracious woman retaineth honour:
and strong men retain riches.

17 The merciful man doeth good
to his own soul: but he that is cruel
troubleth his own flesh.

18 The wicked worketh a deceitful work:
but to him that soweth righteousness
shall be a sure reward.

19 As righteousness tendeth to life:
so he that pursueth evil
pursueth it to his own death.

❦

20 They that are of a froward heart
are abomination to the LORD:
but such as are upright
in their way are his delight.

❦

21 Though hand join in hand, the wicked
shall not be unpunished: but the seed
of the righteous shall be delivered.

❦

22 As a jewel of gold in a swine's snout, so
is a fair woman which is without discretion.

❦

23 The desire of the righteous is only good:
but the expectation of the wicked is wrath.

❦

24 There is that scattereth; ye increaseth;
and there is that withholdeth more than
is meet, but it tendeth to poverty.

Proverbs ❧ 11

25 The liberal soul shall be made fat: and he that watereth shall be watered also himself.

❧

26 He that withholdeth corn, the people shall curse him: but blessing shall be upon the head of him that selleth it.

❧

27 He that diligently seeketh good procureth favour: but he that seeketh mischief, it shall come unto him.

❧

28 He that trusteth in his riches shall fall; but the righteous shall flourish as a branch.

❧

29 He that troubleth his own house shall inherit the wind: and the fool shall be servant to the wise of heart.

❧

30 The fruit of the righteous is a tree of life; and he that winneth souls is wise.

❧

31 Behold, the righteous shall be recompensed in the earth: much more the wicked and the sinner.

12

1 **W**hoso loveth instruction
loveth knowledge:
but he that hateth reproof is brutish

❦

2 **A** good man obtaineth favour of the LORD:
a man of wicked devices will he condemn.

❦

3 **A** man shall not be established by
wickedness: but the root of the
righteous shall not be moved.

❦

4 **A** virtuous woman is a crown to her
husband: but she that maketh ashamed
is as rottenness in his bones.

❦

5 **T**he thoughts of the righteous are right:
but the counsels of the wicked are deceit.

❦

6 **T**he words of the wicked are to lie
in wait for blood: but the mouth of
the upright shall deliver them.

❦

7 **T**he wicked are overthrown, and are not:
but the house of the righteous shall stand.

Proverbs ❦ *12*

8 A man shall be commended according to his wisdom: but he that is of a perverse heart shall be despised.

❦

9 He that is despised, and hath a servant, is better than he that honoureth himself, and lacketh bread.

❦

10 A righteous man regardeth the life of his beast: but the tender mercies of the wicked are cruel.

❦

11 He that tilleth his land shall be satisfied with bread: but he that followeth vain persons is void of understanding.

❦

12 The wicked desireth the net of evil men: but the root of the righteous yieldeth fruit.

❦

13 The wicked is snared by the transgression of his lips: but the just shall come out of trouble.

Proverbs ❧ *12*

14 **A** man shall be satisfied with good
by the fruit of his mouth: and the
recompence of a man's hands shall
be rendered unto him.

❧

15 **T**he way of a fool is right in his own eyes:
but he that hearkeneth to counsel is wise.

❧

16 **A** fool's wrath is presently known:
but a prudent man covereth shame.

❧

17 **H**e that speaketh truth sheweth forth
righteousness: but a false witness deceit.

❧

18 **T**here is that speaketh like the piercings of
a sword: but the tongue of the wise is health.

❧

19 **T**he lip of truth shall be established for
ever: but a lying tongue is but for a moment.

❧

20 **D**eceit is in the heart of them
that imagine evil:
but to the counsellors
of peace is joy.

Proverbs ⁊ *12*

21 There shall no evil happen to the just: but the wicked shall be filled with mischief.

⁊

22 Lying lips are abomination to the LORD: but they that deal truly are his delight.

⁊

23 A prudent man concealeth knowledge: but the heart of fools proclaimeth foolishness.

⁊

24 The hand of the diligent shall bear rule: but the slothful shall be under tribute.

⁊

25 Heaviness in the heart of man maketh it stoop: but a good word maketh it glad.

⁊

26 The righteous is more excellent
than his neighbour:
but the way of the wicked
seduceth them.

⁊

27 The slothful man roasteth not
that which he took in hunting:
but the substance
of a diligent man is precious.

Proverbs ❦ *12*

28 In the way of righteousness
is life: and in the pathway
thereof there is no death.

13

1 A wise son heareth his father's
instruction: but a scorner
heareth not rebuke.

❦

2 A man shall eat good by the fruit of
his mouth: but the soul of the
transgressors shall eat violence.

❦

3 He that keepeth his mouth
keepeth his life: but he that openeth
wide his lips shall have destruction.

❦

4 The soul of the sluggard desireth,
and hath nothing: but the soul of the
diligent shall be made fat.

❦

5 A righteous man hateth lying:
but a wicked man is loathsome,
and cometh to shame.

Proverbs ❦ 13

6 Righteousness keepeth him that is
upright in the way: but wickedness
overthroweth the sinner.

❦

7 There is that maketh himself rich, yet hath
nothing: there is that maketh himself poor,
yet hath great riches.

❦

8 The ransom of a man's life are his riches:
but the poor heareth not rebuke.

❦

9 The light of the righteous rejoiceth: but
the lamp of the wicked shall be put out.

❦

10 Only by pride cometh contention:
but with the well advised is wisdom.

❦

11 Wealth gotten by vanity shall be
diminished: but he that gathereth
by labour shall increase.

❦

12 Hope deferred maketh the heart sick:
but when the desire cometh,
it is a tree of life.

Proverbs ❧ 13

13 **W**hoso despiseth the word shall be destroyed: but he that feareth the commandment shall be rewarded.

❧

14 **T**he law of the wise is a fountain of life, to depart from the snares of death.

❧

15 **G**ood understanding giveth favour: but the way of transgressors is hard.

❧

16 **E**very prudent man dealeth with knowledge: but a fool layeth open his folly.

❧

17 **A** wicked messenger falleth into mischief: but a faithful ambassador is health.

❧

18 **P**overty and shame shall be to him that refuseth instruction: but he that regardeth reproof shall be honoured.

❧

19 **T**he desire accomplished is sweet to the soul: but it is abomination to fools to depart from evil.

Proverbs ❦ *13*

20 He that walketh with wise men
shall be wise: but a companion
of fools shall be destroyed.

❦

21 Evil pursueth sinners: but to the
righteous good shall be repayed.

❦

22 A good man leaveth an inheritance
to his children's children:
and the wealth of the sinner
is laid up for the just.

❦

23 Much food is in the tillage of the
poor: but there is that is destroyed
for want of judgment.

❦

24 He that spareth his rod hateth his
son: but he that loveth him
chasteneth him betimes.

❦

25 The righteous eateth to the
satisfying of his soul: but the belly
of the wicked shall want.

14

1 Every wise woman buildeth
her house: but the foolish
plucketh it down with her hands

🐝

2 He that walketh in his uprightness
feareth the LORD: but he that is
perverse in his ways despiseth him.

🐝

3 In the mouth of the foolish
is a rod of pride: but the lips
of the wise shall preserve them.

🐝

4 Where no oxen are, the crib is clean:
but much increase is by
the strength of the ox.

🐝

5 A faithful witness will not lie:
but a false witness will utter lies.

🐝

6 A scorner seeketh wisdom, and findeth
it not: but knowledge is easy
unto him that understandeth.

Proverbs ⚜ 14

7   Go from the presence of a
foolish man, when thou perceivest
not in him the lips of knowledge.

⚜

8   The wisdom of the prudent
is to understand his way:
but the folly of fools is deceit.

⚜

9   Fools make a mock at sin: but
among the righteous there is favour.

⚜

10   The heart knoweth his own
bitterness; and a stranger doth not
intermeddle with his joy.

⚜

11   The house of the wicked shall be
overthrown: but the tabernacle
of the upright shall flourish.

⚜

12   There is a way which seemeth right
unto a man, but the end thereof
are the ways of death.

Proverbs ❦ 14

13 Even in laughter the heart is sorrowful; and the end of that mirth is heaviness.

❦

14 The backslider in heart shall be filled with his own ways: and a good man shall be satisfied from himself.

❦

15 The simple believeth every word: but the prudent man looketh well to his going.

❦

16 A wise man feareth, and departeth from evil: but the fool rageth, and is confident.

❦

17 He that is soon angry dealeth foolishly: and a man of wicked devices is hated.

❦

18 The simple inherit folly: but the prudent are crowned with knowledge.

❦

19 The evil bow before the good; and the wicked at the gates of the righteous.

Proverbs ☙ 14

20 The poor is hated even of his own
neighbour: but the rich hath many friends.

☙

21 He that despiseth his neighbour sinneth:
but he that hath mercy on the poor,
happy is he.

☙

22 Do they not err that devise evil?
but mercy and truth shall be
to them that devise good.

☙

23 In all labour there is profit: but the talk
of the lips tendeth only to penury.

☙

24 The crown of the wise is their riches:
but the foolishness of fools is folly.

☙

25 A true witness delivereth souls:
but a deceitful witness speaketh lies.

☙

26 In the fear of the LORD is strong
confidence: and his children
shall have a place of refuge.

Proverbs ⚜ 14

27 The fear of the LORD is a fountain of life, to depart from the snares of death.

⚜

28 In the multitude of people is the king's honour: but in the want of people is the destruction of the prince.

⚜

29 He that is slow to wrath is of great understanding: but he that is hasty of spirit exalteth folly.

⚜

30 A sound heart is the life of the flesh: but envy the rottenness of the bones.

⚜

31 He that oppresseth the poor reproacheth his Maker: but he that honoureth him hath mercy on the poor.

⚜

32 The wicked is driven away in his wickedness: but the righteous hath hope in his death.

⚜

33 Wisdom resteth in the heart of him that hath understanding: but that which is in the midst of fools is made known.

34 Righteousness exalteth a nation:
but sin is a reproach to any people.

❧

35 The king's favour is toward
a wise servant: but his wrath
is against him that causeth shame.

15

1 A soft answer turneth away wrath:
but grievous words stir up anger.

❧

2 The tongue of the wise useth
knowledge aright: but the mouth
of fools poureth out foolishness.

❧

3 The eyes of the LORD are in every
place, beholding the evil and the good.

❧

4 A wholesome tongue is a tree of life: but
perverseness therein is a breach in spirit.

❧

5 A fool despiseth his father's
instruction: but he that
regardeth reproof is prudent.

Proverbs 🦢 15

6 In the house of the righteous is much
treasure: but in the revenues of
the wicked is trouble.

🦢

7 The lips of the wise disperse knowledge:
but the heart of the foolish doeth not so.

🦢

8 The sacrifice of the wicked is an
abomination to the LORD: but the
prayer of the upright is his delight.

🦢

9 The way of the wicked is an abomination
unto the LORD: but he loveth him
that followeth after righteousness.

🦢

10 Correction is grievous unto him that
forsaketh the way: and he that
hateth reproof shall die.

🦢

11 Hell and destruction are before
the LORD: how much more then
the hearts of the children of men?

🦢

12 A scorner loveth not one that reproveth
him: neither will he go unto the wise.

Proverbs ⚘ 15

13 **A** merry heart maketh a cheerful
countenance: but by sorrow
of the heart the spirit is broken.

⚘

14 **T**he heart of him that hath understanding
seeketh knowledge: but the mouth of fools
feedeth on foolishness.

⚘

15 **A**ll the days of the afflicted are evil:
but he that is of a merry heart
hath a continual feast.

⚘

16 **B**etter is little with the fear of the LORD
than great treasure and trouble therewith.

⚘

17 **B**etter is a dinner of herbs where love is,
than a stalled ox and hatred therewith.

⚘

18 **A** wrathful man stirreth up strife: but he
that is slow to anger appeaseth strife.

⚘

19 **T**he way of the slothful man
is as an hedge of thorns: but the
way of the righteous is made plain.

Proverbs ❧ 15

20 A wise son maketh a glad father:
but a foolish man despiseth his mother.

❧

21 Folly is joy to him that is destitute
of wisdom: but a man of
understanding walketh uprightly.

❧

22 Without counsel purposes are
disappointed: but in the multitude of
counsellors, they are established.

❧

23 A man hath joy by the answer of
his mouth: and a word spoken

❧

24 The way of life is above to the wise,
that he may depart from hell beneath.

❧

25 The LORD will destroy the house of
the proud: but he will establish
the border of the widow.

❧

26 The thoughts of the wicked are an
abomination to the LORD: but the words
of the pure are pleasant words.

Proverbs ✆ *15*

27 He that is greedy of gain troubleth his
own house; but he that hateth gifts shall live.

28 The heart of the righteous studieth
to answer: but the mouth of the
wicked poureth out evil things.

29 The LORD is far from the wicked: but he
heareth the prayer of the righteous.

30 The light of the eyes rejoiceth the heart:
and a good report maketh the bones fat.

31 The ear that heareth the reproof
of life abideth among the wise.

32 He that refuseth instruction despiseth
his own soul: but he that heareth reproof
getteth understanding.

33 The fear of the LORD is the
instruction of wisdom;
and before honour is humility.

16

1 The preparations of the heart in man,
and the answer of the tongue,
is from the LORD.

2 All the ways of a man are clean in his
own eyes; but the LORD weigheth spirits.

3 Commit thy works unto the LORD,
and thy thoughts shall be established.

4 The LORD hath made all things
for himself: yea, even the wicked for
the day of evil.

5 Every one that is proud in heart
is an abomination to the LORD:
though hand join in hand,
he shall not be unpunished.

6 By mercy and truth iniquity is purged:
and by the fear of the LORD
men depart from evil.

Proverbs ❦ 16

7　**W**hen a man's ways please the LORD,
he maketh even his enemies
to be at peace with him.

❦

8　**B**etter is a little with righteousness
than great revenues without right.

❦

9　**A** man's heart deviseth his way:
but the LORD directeth his steps.

❦

10　**A** divine sentence is in the lips
of the king: his mouth
transgresseth not in judgment.

❦

11　**A** just weight and balance are the LORD's:
all the weights of the bag are his work.

❦

12　**I**t is an abomination to kings
to commit wickedness: for the
throne is established by righteousness.

❦

13　**R**ighteous lips are the delight
of kings; and they love him
that speaketh right.

Proverbs ❧ 16

14 The wrath of a king is as messengers
of death: but a wise man will pacify it.

❧

15 In the light of the king's countenance
is life; and his favour is as a cloud
of the latter rain.

❧

16 How much better is it to get wisdom
than gold! and to get understanding
rather to be chosen than silver!

❧

17 The highway of the upright is to depart
from evil: he that keepeth his way
preserveth his soul.

❧

18 Pride goeth before destruction,
and an haughty spirit before a fall.

❧

19 Better it is to be of an humble spirit
with the lowly, than to divide
the spoil with the proud.

❧

20 Be that handleth a matter wisely
shall find good: and whoso trusteth
in the LORD, happy is he.

Proverbs ☙ 16

21 The wise in heart shall be called
prudent: and the sweetness
of the lips increaseth learning.

22 Understanding is a wellspring of life
unto him that hath it:
but the instruction of fools is folly.

23 The heart of the wise teacheth his
mouth, and addeth learning to his lips.

24 Pleasant words are as a honeycomb,
sweet to the soul,
and health to the bones.

25 There is a way that seemeth right
unto a man, but the end thereof
are the ways of death.

26 He that laboureth laboureth for
himself; for his mouth craveth it of him.

27 An ungodly man diggeth up evil:
and in his lips there is as a burning fire.

Proverbs ❧ 16

28 A froward man soweth strife: and
a whisperer separateth chief friends.

❧

29 A violent man enticeth his neighbour,
and leadeth him into the way
that is not good.

❧

30 He shutteth his eyes to devise
froward things: moving his lips
he bringeth evil to pass.

❧

31 The hoary head is a crown of glory,
if it be found in the way
of righteousness.

❧

32 He that is slow to anger is better
than the mighty; and he that ruleth
his spirit than he that taketh a city.

❧

33 The lot is cast into the lap;
but the whole disposing thereof
is of the LORD.

17

1 **B**etter is a dry morsel, and quietness therewith, than an house full of sacrifices with strife.

2 **A** wise servant shall have rule over a son that causeth shame, and shall have part of the inheritance among the brethren.

3 **T**he fining pot is for silver, and the furnace for gold: but the LORD trieth the hearts.

4 **A** wicked doer giveth heed to false lips; and a liar giveth ear to a naughty tongue.

5 **W**hoso mocketh the poor reproacheth his Maker: and he that is glad at calamities shall not be unpunished.

6 **C**hildren's children are the crown of old men; and the glory of children are their fathers.

Proverbs ❧ 17

7 Excellent speech becometh not a
   fool: much less do lying lips a prince.

8 A gift is as a precious stone
   in the eyes of him that hath it:
   whatever it turneth, it prospereth.

9 He that covereth a transgression
   seeketh love; but he that repeateth
   a matter separateth very friends.

10 A reproof entereth more into
    a wise man than an hundred stripes
    into a fool.

11 An evil man seeketh only rebellion:
    therefore a cruel messenger
    shall be sent against him.

12 Let a bear robbed of her whelps
    meet a man, rather than a fool
    in his folly.

13 Whoso rewardeth evil for good,
    evil shall not depart from his house.

Proverbs 17

14 The beginning of strife is as when
one letteth out water: therefore leave off
contention, before it be meddled with.

15 He that justifieth the wicked, and he that
condemneth the just, even they both are
abomination to the LORD.

16 Wherefore is there a price in the hand
of a fool to get wisdom, seeing he hath
no heart to it?

17 A friend loveth at all times,
and a brother is born for adversity.

18 A man void of understanding
striketh hands, and becometh
surety in the presence of his friend.

19 He loveth transgression that loveth
strife: and he that exalteth his gate
seeketh destruction.

Proverbs ❧ 17

20 **H**e that hath a froward heart
findeth no good: and he that hath a
perverse tongue falleth into mischief.

❧

21 **H**e that begetteth a fool doeth it to
his sorrow: and the father of a fool
hath no joy.

❧

22 **A** merry heart doeth good like
a medicine: but a broken spirit
drieth the bones.

❧

23 **A** wicked man taketh a gift out of the
bosom to pervert the ways of judgment.

❧

24 **W**isdom is before him that hath
understanding; but the eyes
of a fool are in the ends of the earth.

❧

25 **A** foolish son is a grief to his father,
and bitterness to her that bare him.

❧

26 **A**lso to punish the just is not good,
nor to strike princes for equity.

Proverbs ❧ *17*

27 He that hath knowledge spareth his
words: and a man of understanding
is of an excellent spirit.

❧

28 Even a fool, when he holdeth
his peace, is counted wise: and he
that shutteth his lips is esteemed
a man of understanding.

18

1 Through desire a man, having
separated himself, seeketh and
intermeddleth with all wisdom.

❧

2 A fool hath no delight in understanding,
but that his heart may discover itself.

❧

3 When the wicked cometh, then cometh
also contempt, and with ignominy reproach.

❧

4 The words of a man's mouth are
as deep waters, and the wellspring
of wisdom as a flowing brook.

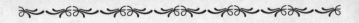

Proverbs ⚜ 18

5 It is not good to accept the person
of the wicked, to overthrow the
righteous in judgment.

⚜

6 A fool's lips enter into contention,
and his mouth calleth for strokes.

⚜

7 A fool's mouth is his destruction,
and his lips are the snare of his soul.

⚜

8 The words of a talebearer are as
wounds, and they go down into
the innermost parts of the belly.

⚜

9 He also that is slothful in his work
is brother to him that is a great waster.

⚜

10 The name of the LORD is a strong
tower: the righteous runneth into it,
and is safe.

⚜

11 The rich man's wealth is his strong city,
and as an high wall in his own conceit.

Proverbs ⚜ 18

12 Before destruction the heart of man is
haughty, and before honour is humility.

⚜

13 He that answereth a matter before he
heareth it, it is folly and shame unto him.

⚜

14 The spirit of a man will sustain his
infirmity; but a wounded spirit
who can bear?

⚜

15 The heart of the prudent getteth
knowledge; and the ear of the wise
seeketh knowledge.

⚜

16 A man's gift maketh room for him,
and bringeth him before great men.

⚜

17 He that is first in his own cause
seemeth just; but his neighbour
cometh and searcheth him.

⚜

18 The lot causeth contentions to cease
and parteth between the mighty.

Proverbs ❧ 18

19 **A** brother offended is harder
to be won than a strong city:
and their contentions are like
the bars of a castle.

❧

20 **A** man's belly shall be satisfied with
the fruit of his mouth; and with the
increase of his lips shall he be filled.

❧

21 **D**eath and life are in the power of
the tongue: and they that love it
shall eat the fruit thereof.

❧

22 **W**hoso findeth a wife findeth
a good thing, and obtaineth favour
of the LORD.

❧

23 **T**he poor useth intreaties;
but the rich answereth roughly.

❧

24 **A** man that hath friends must shew
himself friendly: and there is a friend
that sticketh closer than a brother.

19

1 Better is the poor that walketh in
his integrity, than he that is
perverse in his lips, and is a fool.

2 Also, that the soul be without
knowledge, it is not good; and he
that hasteth with his feet sinneth.

3 The foolishness of man perverteth
his way: and his heart fretteth
against the LORD.

4 Wealth maketh many friends; the
poor is separated from his neighbour.

5 A false witness shall not be
unpunished, and he that
speaketh lies shall not escape.

6 Many will intreat the favour
of the prince: and every man
is a friend to him that giveth gifts.

7 All the brethren of the poor do hate him:
how much more do his friends go far
from him? he pursueth them with words,
yet they are wanting to him.

❧

8 He that getteth wisdom loveth his
own soul: he that keepeth
understanding shall find good.

❧

9 A false witness shall not be unpunished,
and he that speaketh lies shall perish.

❧

10 Delight is not seemly for a fool;
much less for a servant
to have rule over princes.

❧

11 The discretion of a man deferreth
his anger; and it is his glory to
pass over a transgression.

❧

12 The king's wrath is as the roaring
of a lion; but his favour is as dew
upon the grass.

Proverbs ❦ 19

13 A foolish son is the calamity
of his father: and the contentions
of a wife are a continual dropping.

❦

14 House and riches are the inheritance
of fathers: and a prudent wife
is from the LORD.

❦

15 Slothfulness casteth into a deep sleep;
and an idle soul shall suffer hunger.

❦

16 He that keepeth the commandment
keepeth his own soul; but he that
despiseth his ways shall die.

❦

17 He that hath pity upon the poor lendeth
unto the LORD; and that which he hath
given will he pay him again.

❦

18 Chasten thy son while there is hope,
and let not thy soul spare for his crying.

Proverbs ❦ 19

19 A man of great wrath shall suffer punishment: for if thou deliver him, yet thou must do it again.

❦

20 Hear counsel, and receive instruction, that thou mayest be wise in thy latter end.

❦

21 There are many devices in a man's heart; nevertheless the counsel of the LORD, that shall stand.

❦

22 The desire of a man is his kindness: and a poor man is better than a liar.

❦

23 The fear of the LORD tendeth to life: and he that hath it shall abide satisfied; he shall not be visited with evil.

❦

24 A slothful man hideth his hand in his bosom, and will not so much as bring it to his mouth again.

Proverbs ❧ *19*

25 Smite a scorner, and the simple
will beware: and reprove one that
hath understanding, and he will
understand knowledge.

❧

26 He that wasteth his father, and chaseth
away his mother, is a son that
causeth shame, and bringeth reproach.

❧

27 Cease, my son, to hear
the instruction that causeth
to err from the words of knowledge.

❧

28 An ungodly witness scorneth
judgment: and the mouth of the
wicked devoureth iniquity.

❧

29 Judgments are prepared for scorners,
and stripes for the back of fools.

20

1 Wine is a mocker, strong drink
ris aging: and whosoever is deceived
thereby is not wise.

Proverbs ❦ 20

2 The fear of a king is as the roaring
of a lion: whoso provoketh him to
anger sinneth against his own soul.

❦

3 It is an honour for a man to cease from
strife: but every fool will be meddling.

❦

4 The sluggard will not plow by
reason of the cold; therefore shall
he beg in harvest, and have nothing.

❦

5 Counsel in the heart of man is like
deep water; but a man
of understanding will draw it out.

❦

6 Most men will proclaim every one his own
goodness: but a faithful man who can find?

❦

7 The just man walketh in his integrity:
his children are blessed after him.

❦

8 A king that sitteth in the throne
of judgment scattereth away
all evil with his eyes.

Proverbs ⚘ 20

9 Who can say, I have made my heart clean, I am pure from my sin?

⚘

10 Divers weights, and divers measures, both of them are alike abomination to the LORD.

⚘

11 Even a child is known by his doings, whether his work be pure, and whether it be right.

⚘

12 The hearing ear, and the seeing eye, the LORD hath made even both of them.

⚘

13 Love not sleep, lest thou come to poverty; open thine eyes, and thou shalt be satisfied with bread.

⚘

14 It is naught, it is naught, saith the buyer: but when he is gone his way, then he boasteth.

⚘

15 There is gold, and a multitude of rubies: but the lips of knowledge are a precious jewel.

Proverbs ⟡ 20

16 **T**ake his garment that is surety
for a stranger: and take a pledge
of him for a strange woman.

❦

17 **B**read of deceit is sweet to a man;
but afterwards his mouth
shall be filled with gravel.

❦

18 **E**very purpose is established by counsel:
and with good advice make war.

❦

19 **H**e that goeth about as a talebearer
revealeth secrets: therefore meddle not
with him that flattereth with his lips.

❦

20 **W**hoso curseth his father or
his mother, his lamp shall be
put out in obscure darkness.

❦

21 **A**n inheritance may be gotten
hastily at the beginning; but the
end thereof shall not be blessed.

❦

22 **S**ay not thou, I will recompense evil; but
wait on the LORD, and he shall save thee.

Proverbs ⚘ 20

23 Divers weights are an abomination unto the LORD; and a false balance is not good.

⚘

24 Man's goings are of the LORD; how can a man then understand his own way?

⚘

25 It is a snare to the man who devoureth that which is holy, and after vows to make enquiry.

⚘

26 A wise king scattereth the wicked, and bringeth the wheel over them.

⚘

27 The spirit of man is the candle of the LORD, searching all the inward parts of the belly.

⚘

28 Mercy and truth preserve the king: and his throne is upheld by mercy.

⚘

29 The glory of young men is their strength: and the beauty of old men is the grey head.

30 The blueness of a wound
cleanseth away evil: so do stripes
the inward parts of the belly.

21

1 The king's heart is in the hand of
the LORD, as the rivers of water:
he turneth it whithersoever he will.

ꙮ

2 Every way of a man is right
in his own eyes:
but the LORD pondereth the hearts.

ꙮ

3 To do justice and judgment is more
acceptable to the LORD than sacrifice.

ꙮ

4 An high look, and a proud heart,
and the plowing of the wicked, is sin.

ꙮ

5 The thoughts of the diligent tend
only to plenteousness; but of every
one that is hasty only to want.

Proverbs ❧ 21

6 The getting of treasures by a lying
tongue is a vanity tossed to and
fro of them that seek death.

7 The robbery of the wicked
shall destroy them; because they
refuse to do judgment.

8 The way of man is froward and strange:
but as for the pure, his work is right.

9 It is better to dwell in a corner of
the housetop, than with a brawling
woman in a wide house.

10 The soul of the wicked desireth evil:
his neighbour findeth no favour
in his eyes.

11 When the scorner is punished,
the simple is made wise:
and when the wise is instructed,
he receiveth knowledge.

Proverbs ❧ 21

12 The righteous man wisely considereth
the house of the wicked:
but God overthroweth the wicked
for their wickedness.

❧

13 Whoso stoppeth his ears at the cry
of the poor, he also shall cry himself,
but shall not be heard.

❧

14 A gift in secret pacifieth anger: and
a reward in the bosom strong wrath.

❧

15 It is joy to the just to do judgment:
but destruction shall be to the
workers of iniquity.

❧

16 The man that wandereth out of the
way of understanding shall remain
in the congregation of the dead.

❧

17 He that loveth pleasure shall be
a poor man: he that loveth wine
and oil shall not be rich.

Proverbs ❧ 21

18 The wicked shall be a ransom
for the righteous; the transgressor
for the upright.

❧

19 It is better to dwell in the wilderness,
than with a contentious and
an angry woman.

❧

20 There is treasure to be desired
and oil in the dwelling of the wise;
but a foolish man spendeth it up.

❧

21 He that followeth after righteousness
and mercy findeth life, and honour.

❧

22 A wise man scaleth the city of the
mighty, and casteth down the
strength of the confidence thereof.

❧

23 Whoso keepeth his mouth and
tongue keepeth his soul from troubles.

Proverbs ❦ 21

24 Proud and haughty scorner is his
name, who dealeth in proud wrath.

❦

25 The desire of the slothful killeth
him; for his hands refuse to labour.

❦

26 He coveteth greedily all the day long: but
the righteous giveth and spareth not.

❦

27 The sacrifice of the wicked is
abomination: how much more,
when brought with a wicked mind?

❦

28 A false witness shall perish: but the man
that heareth speaketh constantly.

❦

29 A wicked man hardeneth his face:
but as for the upright,
he directeth his way.

❦

30 There is no wisdom, understanding
nor counsel against the LORD.

Proverbs ❧ *21*

31 The horse is prepared against the day of battle: but safety is of the LORD.

22

1 A GOOD name is rather to be chosen than great riches, and loving favour rather than silver and gold.

❧

2 The rich and poor meet together: the LORD is the maker of them all.

❧

3 A prudent man foreseeth the evil, and hideth himself: but the simple pass on, and are punished.

❧

4 By humility and the fear of the LORD are riches, and honour, and life.

❧

5 Thorns and snares are in the way of the froward: he that doth keep his soul shall be far from them.

Proverbs ⚜ 22

6 **T**rain up a child in the way he should go:
and when he is old,
he will not depart from it.

⚜

7 **T**he rich ruleth over the poor,
and the borrower is servant to the lender.

⚜

8 **H**e that soweth iniquity shall reap vanity:
and the rod of his anger shall fail.

⚜

9 **H**e that hath a bountiful eye
shall be blessed; for he giveth
of his bread to the poor.

⚜

10 **C**ast out the scorner, and contention
shall go out; yea, strife and reproach
shall cease.

⚜

11 **H**e that loveth pureness of heart,
for the grace of his lips
the king shall be his friend.

⚜

12 **T**he eyes of the LORD preserve
knowledge, and he overthroweth
the words of the transgressor.

Proverbs ❧ 22

13 The slothful man saith, There is a lion
without, I shall be slain in the streets.

❧

14 The mouth of strange women
is a deep pit: he that is abhorred
of the LORD shall fall therein.

❧

15 Foolishness is bound in the heart
of a child; but the rod of correction
shall drive it far from him.

❧

16 He that oppresseth the poor to increase
his riches, and he that giveth to the rich,
shall surely come to want.

❧

17 Bow down thine ear, and hear the words
of the wise, and apply thine heart
unto my knowledge.

❧

18 For it is a pleasant thing if thou
keep them within thee;
they shall withal be fitted in thy lips.

❧

19 That thy trust may be in the LORD, I have
made known to thee this day, even to thee.

20 Have not I written to thee excellent things
in counsels and knowledge,

☙

21 That I might make thee know
the certainty of the words of truth;
that thou mightest answer the words
of truth to them that send unto thee?

☙

22 Rob not the poor, because he is poor:
neither oppress the afflicted in the gate:

☙

23 For the LORD will plead their cause, and
spoil the soul of those that spoiled them.

☙

24 Make no friendship with an angry man;
and with a furious man thou shalt not go:

☙

25 Lest thou learn his ways,
and get a snare to thy soul.

☙

26 Be not thou one of them that strike hands,
or of them that are sureties for debts.

Proverbs ❧ 22

27 If thou hast nothing to pay, why should
he take away thy bed from under thee?

❧

28 Remove not the ancient landmark,
which thy fathers have set.

❧

29 Seest thou a man diligent in his business?
he shall stand before kings;
he shall not stand before mean men.

23

1 When thou sittest to eat with a ruler,
consider diligently what is before thee:

❧

2 And put a knife to thy throat, if thou
be a man given to appetite.

❧

3 Be not desirous of his dainties:
for they are deceitful meat.

❧

4 Labour not to be rich
cease from thine own wisdom.

5 **W**ilt thou set thine eyes upon that
which is not? for riches certainly make
themselves wings; they fly away
as an eagle toward heaven.

☙

6 **E**at thou not the bread of him that
hath an evil eye, neither desire
thou his dainty meats:

☙

7 **F**or as he thinketh in his heart, so is he:
Eat and drink, saith he to thee;
but his heart is not with thee.

☙

8 **T**he morsel which thou hast eaten shalt
thou vomit up, and lose thy sweet words.

☙

9 **S**peak not in the ears of a fool: for he
will despise the wisdom of thy words.

☙

10 **R**emove not the old landmark; and enter
not into the fields of the fatherless:

☙

11 **F**or their redeemer is mighty;
he shall plead their cause with thee.

Proverbs 23

12 **A**pply thine heart unto instruction,
and thine ears to the words of knowledge.

13 **W**ithhold not correction from the child:
for if thou beatest him with the rod,
he shall not die.

14 **T**hou shalt beat him with the rod,
and shalt deliver his soul from hell.

15 **M**y son, if thine heart be wise,
my heart shall rejoice, even mine.

16 **Y**ea, my reins shall rejoice,
when thy lips speak right things.

17 **L**et not thine heart envy sinners:
but be thou in the fear of the LORD
all the day long.

18 **F**or surely there is an end; and thine
expectation shall not be cut off.

Proverbs ᠅ 23

19 Hear thou, my son, and be wise,
and guide thine heart in the way.

᠅

20 Be not among winebibbers;
among riotous eaters of flesh:

᠅

21 For the drunkard and the glutton shall
come to poverty: and drowsiness shall
clothe a man with rags.

᠅

22 Hearken unto thy father that begat thee,
and despise not thy mother when she is old.

᠅

23 Buy the truth, and sell it not; also wisdom,
and instruction, and understanding.

᠅

24 The father of the righteous shall
greatly rejoice: and he that begetteth
a wise child shall have joy of him.

᠅

25 Thy father and thy mother shall be glad,
and she that bare thee shall rejoice.

Proverbs ॐ 23

26 **M**y son, give me thine heart,
  and let thine eyes observe my ways.

ॐ

27 **F**or a whore is a deep ditch;
  and a strange woman is a narrow pit.

ॐ

28 **S**he also lieth in wait as for a prey, and
  increaseth the transgressors among men.

ॐ

29 **W**ho hath woe? who hath sorrow?
  who hath contentions? who hath
  babbling? who hath wounds without
  cause? who hath redness of eyes?

ॐ

30 **T**hey that tarry long at the wine;
  they that go to seek mixed wine.

ॐ

31 **L**ook not thou upon the wine when
  it is red, when it giveth his colour
  in the cup, when it moveth itself aright.

ॐ

32 **A**t the last it biteth like a serpent,
  and stingeth like an adder.

33 Thine eyes shall behold strange women,
and thine heart shall utter perverse things.

❦

34 Yea, thou shalt be as he that lieth down
in the midst of the sea, or as he that
lieth upon the top of a mast.

❦

35 They have stricken me, shalt thou say,
and I was not sick; they have beaten me,
and I felt it not: when shall I awake?
I will seek it yet again.

24

1 Be not thou envious against evil men,
neither desire to be with them.

❦

2 For their heart studieth destruction,
and their lips talk of mischief.

❦

3 Through wisdom is an house builded;
and by understanding it is established:

❦

4 And by knowledge shall the chambers be
filled with all precious and pleasant riches.

Proverbs ⚘ 24

5   A wise man is strong; yea, a man
of knowledge increaseth strength.

⚘

6   For by wise counsel thou shalt make
thy war: and in multitude of counsellors
there is safety.

⚘

7   Wisdom is too high for a fool:
he openeth not his mouth in the gate.

⚘

8   He that deviseth to do evil
shall be called a mischievous person.

⚘

9   The thought of foolishness is sin: and
the scorner is an abomination to men.

⚘

10   If thou faint in the day of adversity,
thy strength is small.

⚘

11   If thou forbear to deliver them
that are drawn unto death,
and those that are ready to be slain;

Proverbs ❧ 24

12 **I**f thou sayest, Behold, we knew it not;
doth not he that pondereth the heart
consider it? and he that keepeth thy soul,
doth not he know it? and shall not he
render to every man according to his works?

❧

13 **M**y son, eat thou honey, because
it is good; and the honeycomb,
which is sweet to thy taste:

❧

14 **S**o shall the knowledge of wisdom
be unto thy soul: when thou hast
found it, then there shall be a reward,
and thy expectation shall not be cut off.

❧

15 **L**ay not wait, O wicked man,
against the dwelling of the righteous;
spoil not his resting place:

❧

16 **F**or a just man falleth seven times,
and riseth up again: but the wicked
shall fall into mischief.

❧

17 **R**ejoice not when thine enemy falleth,
and let not thine heart be glad
when he stumbleth:

Proverbs ❧ 24

18 Lest the LORD see it, and it displease him
and he turn away his wrath from him.

❧

19 Fret not thyself because of evil men,
neither be thou envious at the wicked:

❧

20 For there shall be no reward to the evil man;
the candle of the wicked shall be put out.

❧

21 My son, fear thou the LORD and the king:
and meddle not with them that
are given to change:

❧

22 For their calamity shall rise suddenly;
and who knoweth the ruin of them both?

❧

23 These things also belong to the wise.
It is not good to have respect of
persons in judgment.

❧

24 He that saith unto the wicked,
'Thou are righteous; him shall the
people curse, nations shall abhor him:'

25 **B**ut to them that rebuke him
shall be delight, and a good blessing
shall come upon them.

🌿

26 **E**very man shall kiss his lips
that giveth a right answer.

🌿

27 **P**repare thy work without, and make it
fit for thyself in the field; and afterwards
build thine house.

🌿

28 **B**e not a witness against thy neighbour
without cause; deceive not with thy lips.

🌿

29 **S**ay not, I will do so to him as he hath
done to me: I will render to the man
according to his work.

🌿

30 **I** went by the field of the slothful,
and by the vineyard of the man
void of understanding;

Proverbs ❧ 24

31 And, lo, it was all grown over with thorns,
and nettles had covered the face thereof,
the stone wall thereof was broken down.

32 Then I saw, and considered it well:
I looked upon it, and received instruction.

33 Yet a little sleep, a little slumber,
a little folding of the hands to sleep:

34 So shall thy poverty come as one that
travelleth; and thy want as an armed man.

25

1 These are also proverbs of Solomon,
which the men of Hezekiah,
king of Judah copied out.

2 It is the glory of God to conceal a thing:
but the honour of kings is to search
out a matter.

Proverbs ❧ 25

3 The heaven for height, and the earth
for depth, and the heart of kings
is unsearchable.

❧

4 Take away the dross from the silver,
and there shall come forth a vessel
for the finer.

❧

5 Take away the wicked from before
the king, and his throne shall be
established in righteousness.

❧

6 Put not forth thyself in the presence
of the king, and stand not
in the place of great men:

❧

7 For better it is that it be said unto thee,
Come up hither; than that thou shouldest
be put lower in the presence of the prince
whom thine eyes have seen.

❧

8 Go not forth hastily to strive, lest thou
know not what to do in the end thereof,
when thy neighbour hath put thee to shame.

Proverbs ❧ 25

9 Debate thy cause with thy
neighbor himself; and discover not
a secret to another:

❧

10 Lest he that heareth it put thee to shame,
and thine infamy turn not away.

❧

11 A word fitly spoken is like apples of gold
in pictures of silver.

❧

12 As an earring of gold, and an ornament
of fine gold, so is a wise reprover upon
an obedient ear.

❧

13 As the cold of snow in the time of harvest,
so is a faithful messenger to them that
send him: for he refresheth the soul
of his masters.

❧

14 Whoso boasteth himself of a false gift
is like clouds and wind without rain.

❧

15 By long forbearing is a prince persuaded,
and a soft tongue breaketh the bone.

Proverbs ❦ 25

16 Hast thou found honey? eat so much
as is sufficient for thee, lest thou
be filled therewith, and vomit it.

❦

17 Withdraw thy foot from thy neighbour's
house; lest he be weary of thee,
and so hate thee.

❦

18 A man that beareth false witness
against his neighbour is a maul,
and a sword, and a sharp arrow.

❦

19 Confidence in an unfaithful man
in time of trouble is like a broken tooth,
and a foot out of joint.

❦

20 As he that taketh away a garment in cold
weather, and as vinegar upon nitre, so is
he that singeth songs to an heavy heart.

❦

21 If thine enemy be hungry, give him
bread to eat; and if he be thirsty,
give him water to drink:

Proverbs ⚘ 25

22 For thou shalt heap coals of fire upon
his head, and the LORD shall reward thee.

⚘

23 The north wind driveth away rain:
so doth an angry countenance
a backbiting tongue.

⚘

24 It is better to dwell in the corner of the
housetop, than with a brawling woman
and in a wide house.

⚘

25 As cold waters to a thirsty soul,
so is good news from a far country.

⚘

26 A righteous man falling down
before the wicked is as a troubled
fountain, and a corrupt spring.

⚘

27 It is not good to eat much honey:
so for men to search their own glory
is not glory.

⚘

28 He that hath no rule over his own spirit
is like a city that is broken down,
and without walls.

26

1 As snow in summer, and as rain
in harvest, so honour is not seemly
for a fool.

※

2 As the bird by wandering,
as the swallow by flying, so the curse
causeless shall not come.

※

3 A whip for the horse, a bridle for the ass,
and a rod for the fool's back.

※

4 Answer not a fool according to his folly,
lest thou also be like unto him.

※

5 Answer a fool according to his folly,
lest he be wise in his own conceit.

※

6 He that sendeth a message by
the hand of a fool cutteth off the feet,
and drinketh damage.

※

7 The legs of the lame are not equal:
so is a parable in the mouth of fools.

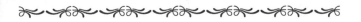

Proverbs ⚘ 26

8 As he that bindeth a stone in a sling,
so is he that giveth honour to a fool.

⚘

9 As a thorn goeth up into the hand of
a drunkard, so is a parable
in the mouths of fools.

⚘

10 The great God that formed all things
both rewardeth the fool,
and rewardeth transgressors.

⚘

11 As a dog returneth to his vomit,
so a fool returneth to his folly.

⚘

12 Seest thou a man wise in his own conceit?
there is more hope of a fool than of him.

⚘

13 The slothful man saith, There is a lion
in the way; a lion is in the streets.

⚘

14 As the door turneth upon his hinges,
so doth the slothful upon his bed.

15 The slothful hideth his hand in his bosom;
it grieveth him to bring it again to his mouth.

❧

16 The sluggard is wiser in his own conceit
than seven men that can render a reason.

❧

17 He that passeth by, and meddleth with
strife belonging not to him, is like one
that taketh a dog by the ears.

❧

18 As a mad man who casteth firebrands,
arrows, and death,

❧

19 So is the man that deceiveth his
neighbour, and saith, Am not I in sport?

❧

20 Where no wood is, there the fire
goeth out: so where there is no talebearer,
the strife ceaseth.

❧

21 As coals are to burning coals, and wood
to fire; so is a contentious man
to kindle strife.

Proverbs 26

22 The words of a talebearer are as wounds, and they go down into the innermost parts of the belly.

23 Burning lips and a wicked heart are like a potsherd covered with silver dross.

24 He that hateth dissembleth with his lips, and layeth up deceit within him;

25 When he speaketh fair, believe him not: for there are seven abominations in his heart.

26 Whose hatred is covered by deceit, his wickedness shall be shewed before the whole congregation.

27 Whoso diggeth a pit shall fall therein: and he that rolleth a stone, it will return upon him.

28 A lying tongue hateth those that are afflicted by it; and a flattering mouth worketh ruin.

27

1 **B**oast not thyself of to morrow; for thou knowest not what a day may bring forth.

❦

2 **L**et another man praise thee,
and not thine own mouth;
a stranger, and not thine own lips.

❦

3 **A** stone is heavy, and the sand weighty;
but a fool's wrath is heavier
than them both.

❦

4 **W**rath is cruel, and anger is outrageous;
but who is able to stand before envy?

❦

5 **O**pen rebuke is better than secret love.

❦

6 **F**aithful are the wounds of a friend;
but the kisses of an enemy are deceitful.

❦

7 **T**he full soul loatheth an honeycomb;
but to the hungry soul
every bitter thing is sweet.

Proverbs ❧ 27

8 As a bird that wandereth from her nest,
so is a man that wandereth from his place.

❧

9 Ointment and perfume rejoice the heart:
so doth the sweetness of a man's friend
by hearty counsel.

❧

10 Thine own friend, and thy father's friend,
forsake not; neither go into thy brother's
house in the day of thy calamity:
for better is a neighbour that is near
than a brother far off.

❧

11 My son, be wise, and make my heart glad,
that I may answer him that reproacheth me.

❧

12 A prudent man foreseeth the evil,
and hideth himself; but the simple
pass on, and are punished.

❧

13 Take his garment that is surety
for a stranger, and take a pledge
of him for a strange woman.

Proverbs ❧ 27

14 He that blesseth his friend with a loud
voice, rising early in the morning,
it shall be counted a curse to him.

❧

15 A continual dropping in a very rainy day
and a contentious woman are alike.

❧

16 Whosoever hideth her hideth the wind,
and the ointment of his right hand,
which bewrayeth itself.

❧

17 Iron sharpeneth iron; so a man
sharpeneth the countenance of his friend.

❧

18 Whoso keepeth the fig tree shall eat
the fruit thereof: so he that waiteth
on his master shall be honoured.

❧

19 As in water face answereth to face,
so the heart of man to man.

❧

20 Hell and destruction are never full;
so the eyes of man are never satisfied.

Proverbs ॐ 27

21 As the fining pot for silver, and the furnace for gold; so is a man to his praise.

ॐ

22 Though thou shouldest bray a fool
in a mortar among wheat with a pestle,
yet will not his foolishness depart from him.

ॐ

23 Be thou diligent to know the state of thy flocks, and look well to thy herds.

ॐ

24 For riches are not for ever: and doth the crown endure to every generation?

ॐ

25 The hay appeareth, and the tender grass sheweth itself, and herbs of the mountains are gathered.

ॐ

26 The lambs are for thy clothing, and the goats are the price of the field.

ॐ

27 And thou shalt have goats' milk enough for thy food, for the food of thy household, and for the maintenance for thy maidens.

28

1 The wicked flee when no man pursueth:
but the righteous are bold as a lion.

2 For the transgression of a land many are
the princes thereof: but by a man of
understanding and knowledge the state
thereof shall be prolonged.

3 A poor man that oppresseth the poor is
like a sweeping rain which leaveth no food.

4 They that forsake the law praise the
wicked: but such as keep the law
contend with them.

5 Evil men understand not judgment:
but they that seek the LORD
understand all things.

6 Better is the poor that walketh in his
uprightness, than he that is perverse
in his ways, though he be rich.

Proverbs ❧ 28

7 **W**hoso keepeth the law is a wise son:
but he that is a companion of
riotous men shameth his father.

❧

8 **H**e that by usury and unjust gain
increaseth his substance, he shall
gather it for him that will pity the poor.

❧

9 **H**e that turneth away his ear from
hearing the law, even his prayer
shall be abomination.

❧

10 **W**hoso causeth the righteous to go astray
in an evil way, he shall fall himself into
his own pit: but the upright shall have
good things in possession.

❧

11 **T**he rich man is wise in his own conceit;
but the poor that hath understanding
searcheth him out.

❧

12 **W**hen righteous men do rejoice,
there is great glory: but when the
wicked rise, a man is hidden.

Proverbs 28

13 He that covereth his sins shall not
prosper: but whoso confesseth
and forsaketh them shall have mercy.

❦

14 Happy is the man that feareth alway:
but he that hardeneth his heart
shall fall into mischief.

❦

15 As a roaring lion, and a ranging bear;
so is a wicked ruler over the poor people.

❦

16 The prince that wanteth understanding
is also a great oppressor: but he that
hateth covetousness shall prolong his days.

❦

17 A man that doeth violence to the blood
of any person shall flee to the pit;
let no man stay him.

❦

18 Whoso walketh uprightly shall be saved:
but he that is perverse in his ways
shall fall at once.

Proverbs ❦ 28

19 He that tilleth his land shall have plenty of bread: but he that followeth after vain persons shall have poverty enough.

❦

20 A faithful man shall abound with blessings: but he that maketh haste to be rich shall not be innocent.

❦

21 To have respect of persons is not good: or for a piece of bread that man will transgress.

❦

22 He that hasteth to be rich hath an evil eye, and considereth not that poverty shall come upon him.

❦

23 He that rebuketh a man afterwards shall find more favour than he that flattereth with the tongue.

❦

24 Whoso robbeth his father or his mother, and saith, It is no transgression; the same is the companion of a destroyer.

Proverbs ☞ 28

25 He that is of a proud heart stirreth up
strife: but he that putteth his trust
in the LORD shall be made fat.

☞

26 He that trusteth in his own heart
is a fool: but whoso walketh wisely,
he shall be delivered.

☞

27 He that giveth unto the poor
shall not lack: but he that hideth
his eyes shall have many a curse.

☞

28 When the wicked rise, men hide
themselves: but when they perish,
the righteous increase.

29

1 He, that being often reproved hardeneth
his neck, shall suddenly be destroyed,
and that without remedy.

☞

2 When the righteous are in authority,
the people rejoice: but when the
wicked beareth rule, the people mourn.

Proverbs ❧ 29

3 Whoso loveth wisdom rejoiceth
his father: but he that keepeth company
with harlots spendeth his substance.

4 The king by judgment establisheth
the land: but he that receiveth gifts
overthroweth it.

5 A man that flattereth his neighbour
spreadeth a net for his feet.

6 In the transgression of an evil man
there is a snare: but the righteous
doth sing and rejoice.

7 The righteous considereth the cause
of the poor: but the wicked regardeth
not to know it.

8 Scornful men bring a city into a snare:
but wise men turn away wrath.

9 If a wise man contendeth with a foolish
man, whether he rage or laugh,
there is no rest.

Proverbs ❧ 29

10 The bloodthirsty hate the upright:
but the just seek his soul.

❧

11 A fool uttereth all his mind: but a wise
man keepeth it in till afterwards.

❧

12 If a ruler hearken to lies,
all his servants are wicked.

❧

13 The poor and the deceitful man meet
together: the LORD lighteneth
both their eyes.

❧

14 The king that faithfully judgeth the poor,
his throne shall be established for ever.

❧

15 The rod and reproof give wisdom:
but a child left to himself
bringeth his mother to shame.

❧

16 When the wicked are multiplied,
transgression increaseth:
but the righteous shall see their fall.

Proverbs ❦ 29

17 Correct thy son, and he shall give thee rest; yea, he shall give delight unto thy soul.

❦

18 Where there is no vision, the people perish: but he that keepeth the law, happy is he.

❦

19 A servant will not be corrected by words: though he understand he will not answer.

❦

20 Seest thou a man that is hasty in his words? there is more hope of a fool than of him.

❦

21 He that delicately bringeth up his servant from a child shall have him become his son at the length.

❦

22 An angry man stirreth up strife, and a furious man aboundeth in transgression.

❦

23 A man's pride shall bring him low: but honour shall uphold the humble in spirit.

Proverbs ❦ 29

24 Whoso is partner with a thief hateth
his own soul: he heareth cursing,
and bewrayeth it not.

❦

25 The fear of man bringeth a snare:
but whoso putteth his trust
in the LORD shall be safe.

❦

26 Many seek the ruler's favour; but every
man's judgment cometh from the LORD.

❦

27 An unjust man is an abomination
to the just: and he that is upright
in the way is abomination to the wicked.

30

1 The words of Agur the son of Jakeh,
even the prophecy: the man spake
unto Ithiel, even unto Ithiel and Ucal,

❦

2 Surely I am more brutish than any man,
and have not the understanding of a man.

Proverbs ❦ 30

3 I neither learned wisdom,
nor have the knowledge of the holy.

❦

4 Who hath ascended up into heaven,
or descended? who hath gathered the
wind in his fists? who hath bound the
waters in a garment? who hath
established all the ends of the earth?
what is his name, and what is his
son's name, if thou canst tell?

❦

5 Every word of God is pure: he is a shield
unto them that put their trust in him.

❦

6 Add thou not unto his words, lest he
reprove thee, and thou be found a liar.

❦

7 Two things have I required of thee;
deny me them not before I die:

❦

8 Remove far from me vanity and lies:
give me neither poverty nor riches;
feed me with food convenient for me:

Proverbs ❦ 30

9 Lest I be full, and deny thee, and say,
Who is the LORD? or lest I be poor,
and steal, and take the name
of my God in vain.

❦

10 Accuse not a servant unto his master,
lest he curse thee, and thou be found guilty.

❦

11 There is a generation that curseth their
father, and doth not bless their mother.

❦

12 There is a generation that are pure
in their own eyes, and yet is not
washed from their filthiness.

❦

13 There is a generation, O how lofty are
their eyes! and their eyelids are lifted up.

❦

14 There is a generation, whose teeth
are as swords, and their jaw teeth
as knives, to devour the poor from
off the earth, and the needy
from among men.

Proverbs ❧ 30

15 The horseleach hath two daughters,
crying, Give, give. There are three
things that are never satisfied, yea,
four things say not, It is enough:

16 The grave; and the barren womb;
the earth that is not filled with water;
and the fire that saith not, It is enough.

17 The eye that mocketh at his father,
and despiseth to obey his mother,
the ravens of the valley shall pick it out,
and the young eagles shall eat it.

18 There be three things which are
too wonderful for me,
yea, four which I know not:

19 The way of an eagle in the air;
the way of a serpent upon a rock;
the way of a ship in the midst of the sea;
and the way of a man with a maid.

20 Such is the way of an adulterous woman;
she eateth, and wipeth her mouth, and
saith, I have done no wickedness.

Proverbs ⚡ 30

21 For three things the earth is disquieted,
and for four which it cannot bear:

⚡

22 For a servant when he reigneth;
and a fool when he is filled with meat;

⚡

23 For an odious woman when she
is married; and an handmaid that
is heir to her mistress.

⚡

24 There be four things which are little upon
the earth, but they are exceeding wise:

⚡

25 The ants are a people not strong, yet
they prepare their meat in the summer;

⚡

26 The conies are but a feeble folk,
yet make they their houses in the rocks;

⚡

27 The locusts have no king,
yet go they forth all of them by bands;

⚡

28 The spider taketh hold with her hands,
and is in kings' palaces.

Proverbs ❦ 30

29 There be three things which go well,
yea, four are comely in going:

❦

30 A lion which is strongest among beasts,
and turneth not away for any;

❦

31 A greyhound; an he goat also; and a king,
against whom there is no rising up.

❦

32 If thou hast done foolishly in lifting up
thyself, or if thou hast thought evil,
lay thine hand upon thy mouth.

❦

33 Surely the churning of milk bringeth
forth butter, and the wringing of the
nose bringeth forth blood: so the
forcing of wrath bringeth forth strife.

31

1 The words of king Lemuel, the prophecy
that his mother taught him.

❦

2 What, my son? and what, the son of my
womb? and what, the son of my vows?

Proverbs ☙ 31

3 Give not thy strength unto women, nor
thy ways to that which destroyeth kings.

☙

4 It is not for kings, O Lemuel,
it is not for kings to drink wine;
nor for princes strong drink:

☙

5 Lest they drink, and forget the law,
and pervert the judgment of any
of the afflicted.

☙

6 Give strong drink unto him that is
ready to perish, and wine unto those
that be of heavy hearts.

☙

7 Let him drink, and forget his poverty,
and remember his misery no more.

☙

8 Open thy mouth for the dumb
in the cause of all such
as are appointed to destruction.

☙

9 Open thy mouth, judge righteously, and
plead the cause of the poor and needy.

Proverbs ❧ 31

10 **W**ho can find a virtuous woman?
for her price is far above rubies.

❧

11 **T**he heart of her husband
doth safely trust in her,
so that he shall have no need of spoil.

❧

12 **S**he will do him good and not evil
all the days of her life.

❧

13 **S**he seeketh wool, and flax,
and worketh willingly with her hands.

❧

14 **S**he is like the merchants' ships;
she bringeth her food from afar.

❧

15 **S**he riseth also while it is yet night,
and giveth meat to her household,
and a portion to her maidens.

❧

16 **S**he considereth a field, and buyeth it:
with the fruit of her hands
she planteth a vineyard.

Proverbs ✾ 31

17 She girdeth her loins with strength,
and strengtheneth her arms.

✾

18 She perceiveth that her merchandise is
good: her candle goeth not out by night.

✾

19 She layeth her hands to the spindle,
and her hands hold the distaff.

✾

20 She stretchout her hand to the poor; yea,
she reacheth forth her hands to the needy.

✾

21 She is not afraid of the snow for her
household: for all her household are
clothed with scarlet.

✾

22 She maketh herself coverings of tapestry;
her clothing is silk and purple.

✾

23 Her husband is known in the gates, when
he sitteth among the elders of the land.

✾

24 She maketh fine linen, and selleth it;
and delivereth girdles unto the merchant.

Proverbs ❧ 31

25 Strength and honour are her clothing;
and she shall rejoice in time to come.

❧

26 She openeth her mouth with wisdom;
and in her tongue is the law of kindness.

❧

27 She looketh well to the ways of her
household, and eateth not the
bread of idleness.

❧

28 Her children arise up, and call her
blessed; her husband also,
and he praiseth her.

❧

29 Many daughters have done virtuously,
but thou excellest them all.

❧

30 Favour is deceitful, and beauty is vain:
but a woman that feareth the LORD,
she shall be praised.

❧

31 Give her of the fruit of her hands;
and let her own works
praise her in the gates.

Reflections

~ *Reflections* ~

~ Reflections ~